By the Light of the Moon

Written by AC Yates

By the Light of the Moon

Copyright © 2020 AC Yates

All rights reserved. No part of this publication may be reproduced, stored in a retrieval system, or transmitted in any form or by any means, electronic, mechanical, photocopying, recording or otherwise, without the prior written permission from both the copyright owner and publisher.

ISBN: 9798583465446

I feel in every girl
there lives
a wild pixie,
that if let go,
would run and dance in grassy fields
until the end of the world
and when that girl grows up,
that pixie hides,
but she's always there,
peeking out behind old eyes
and reading glasses,
waiting
to one day dance again.

~ Atticus

I dedicate this book to you, Katey Roberts.
For seeing something inside me that I couldn't see.
For your guidance and constant encouragement to face the fear and vulnerability, and do it anyway.

Thank you for making this happen

To each and every one of you
Who have spurred me on through the writing of my book
Who convinced me I could
When I convinced myself I couldn't
I completely honour you
From the love in my heart to the love that's in yours

A Message From Annie

I was born and bred up North in a little town called Bolton. I have two wonderful children and two beautiful Granddaughters.

I am a hairdresser, holistic therapist, Reiki master, and now an author of a poetry book. I never ever imagined in my wildest dreams that I would write a book and have it published, let alone a poetry book.

I hated writing at school – I was always the one sat at the back of the class chatting. Then, last year, I joined a Facebook writing group run by the lovely Katey Roberts called *Love, What Would You Have Me Know* and everything changed! Now, I love writing, and always have a note book and pen with me, just in case I get a little inspiration.

Most of my writing I did at night, once I got into bed. The nights when I couldn't sleep I would sit on my bed by the light of the moon and write – that's where the title came from.

Some of my poems are imaginary, others are about real life

and truth. They all come from the heart, and all of them are written with love as my guide.

I hope you enjoy my book. Who knows, it may even inspire you to write too!

Love Annie ♡

Contents

1. Love..1
2. Me..2
3. September.......................................5
4. The Stalker.....................................7
5. Just A Memory...............................9
6. A Nice Hot Bath 11
7. Water Love 13
8. Goodbye Mum..............................15
9. You Made My Day 17
10. Nothing Has Changed................19
11. Romantic Day For One 22
12. The Scary Path 24
13. The Raven...................................26
14. No Fear 28
15. Oh, To Be A Woman 30
16. My Girl...32
17. Willow..34
18. Just A Little Walk 35
19. The Visitor 37
20. My Boy..39
21. A Stolen Moment 41

22. All Hallows Eve	43
23. The Dream	45
24. Florence	48
25. The Storm	50
26. Perfect Timing	52
27. Messages From Love	53
28. Spring Equinox	55
29. To-Do List	57
30. Beautiful Women	59
31. So Ill	61
32. Lucky To Be Here	63
33. Morning Gratitude	66
34. We Are One	68
35. Message From A Friend	69
36. Not Today	71
37. The Break Up	73
38. I'm Just Tired	75
39. A Mother's Love	76
40. The Funeral	77
41. The Little Things	80
42. Unconditional Love	82
43. Mixed Bag	84
44. Free Spirit	85
45. November	87
46. Our Jinx	88

47. Full Moon	89
48. The Great Oak Tree	90
49. An Ode To Mr Fly	91
50. Listen To Love	93
51. My Birthday	96
52. My Beautiful Love And Me	98
53. Time To Go	99
54. I'm Grounded	101
55. Dance With Me Love	103
56. Dreamy Day In Cyprus	105
57. My Beating Heart	107
58. Bonfire Night	108
59. Luscious Lips	110
60. Strange Feelings	112
61. Go With The Flow	114
62. Drifting Off	115
63. Fragile	117
64. Anxiety	118
65. I Shouldn't Be Here	120
66. Time	121
67. Sadness	122
68. Summer's End	124

1.
Love

Love is me

Love is you

Love is all around us

Love is inside us

It's in our voice

How we speak our words

How we speak our truth

It's in our heart and how we feel love

We radiate love

We are love

Open your eyes and allow love to guide the way ♡

2.
Me

I am Ann!
Hebrew meaning
He (God) has favoured me,
Gracious and merciful.
Most people call me Annie which I prefer
Though my mum would not approve.
I'm a passenger on this journey of life
Being guided by love.
A student of universal life lessons.

I'm not perfect, I've made mistakes
But I have learnt and I'm still learning that
Truth and honesty are paramount.
I may appear quiet and shy,
But I'm not.
I'm probably just getting the measure of things.
I'm sensitive and emotional to the point of frustration.
I'm compassionate and loving.
When I love you I will love you forever.
I'm learning to forgive those who wound me,

Their doing is not my lesson to learn.
I'm a peace maker,
Never a fighter –
Sometimes this can make me appear weak,
But I'm stronger than I look.
I don't judge, we are all the same.
Nor will I speak ill of you –
I don't want the karma.
I'm learning to let go of the external validation,
And avoid those who steal my energy.
Some days, I barely have enough energy for myself.
I sometimes doubt that I'm loved,
Though I know I am.
I'm learning to love and accept my imperfect self.
I no longer hide in the dark shadows of my past –
I am a survivor and a warrior.

I love to spend time alone, though I'm not a loner.
Being out in nature amongst the vegetation and trees is bliss to me.
Or by the open water, though I would never venture in it.
My earth connection and my roots are strong.
I'm at home and at peace with Mother Earth.

I'm in awe of the moon,

A star gazer,

A cloud bather.

The whole universe flows through me

Love in its entirety ♡

3.
September

Beautiful September,
Do you know how much I love you?
My favourite month of all.
I love the changes that you bring,
The last few days of summer falling at your feet.

The changing colours of the trees,
Leaves losing their grip on life fluttering at my feet.
Vibrant shades of amber, orange, crimson and brown
Once again exposing the autumn landscape,
The wondrous hills how they rise and fall.

The fragrant air smells different too,
More woody,
Stronger scents of cedarwood and pine,
More earthy tones, musky and fresh,
Awakening my senses with every breath.

The morning dew much damper and heavier
Bringing with it an autumn mist,

Forming tiny pearly beads on barely visible spiderwebs
So intricately made
Like delicate pieces woven lace.

Feeling the slight fresh cooling nip in the air
My skin welcomes it with glee.
Winter isn't too far away now.
How I love you winter!
The sun much lower in the autumn sky,
The sunsets more vibrant setting the sky alight.

Shorter days, longer, darker nights.
Oh, I love the dark nights!
Close the curtains and settle down,
Cosy evenings by the cracking fire,
Getting lost in the dancing flames and burning embers.
Glowing faces, toasty warm toes.

I feel blessed with love to have been September born
On the very last day of my beautiful favourite month. ♡

4.
The Stalker

I notice you are here again,
Same time every morning.
You never fail to appear
Come rain or sunshine.

Hiding behind my neighbour's fence,
Peeping through the bushes at them,
Silently watching
Waiting
Ready to pounce
On your unsuspecting victim.

Will today be their fateful day?

What are you planning?
Is it just curiosity?
Are you going to attack and leave your victim for dead?
Do you intend to kill them in cold blood?
Will you capture them and take them with you,
Leaving the scene of the crime?

You don't know I'm watching you watching them,
Even if you did it wouldn't stop you.

Suddenly, a creaking door opens.
It scares you.
You attack anyway,
Throwing yourself at the mercy of the bushes
Hoping for a catch
Or just a taste.
But the birds are onto you pussy cat
As they all make their escape
Tweeting,
Warning each other of the stalker's presence.

5.
Just a Memory

I haven't seen you for such a long time –
I've missed you more than you know.
If I close my eyes I can imagine you standing there before me
As large as life,
Smiling your beautiful smile.
Your twinkling eyes,
The way you gave me that loving stare.
Hold me in your arms just one more time,
I need to feel you close.
My face pressed on your chest
I can feel your heart racing.
You smell as sweet as I remember –
Fresh, clean and musky.
It's lovely being in your arms again
Even if it is just in my head.
I'm scared to open my eyes –
What if you disappear,
Gone forever?
What if I forget what you look like?

I want to stay here, just a few minutes more.
I open my eyes and you're gone,
Back in my memory
Until we meet again. ♡

6.
A Nice Hot Bath

I put in the plug and turn on the tap.

It's time for some long awaited self-love.

It was a dark cold evening,

The heating was on,

My fluffy towel was warming on the radiator.

Soft music was playing in the background

I lit the candles and placed them round the bath.

It looked like a sacrificial offering,

Well, it was to myself.

I sat on the edge of the tub, watching the water

Splashing and crackling like a thunderous waterfall.

Stirring it occasionally with my fingertips,

Hot but blissful against my skin.

The steam forming droplets on my face.

My senses are starting to come alive,

An added intoxicating aroma of oils that are starting to infuse.

The aromatic spicy warm smell of ginger

And the musky earthy smell of patchouli.

They take me back to my childhood hippy days

When life was simple.

I dip my toes,

They tingle at the heat.

Soon I am engulfed

In a tub full of ecstasy.

It's hot but divine.

My head and face are submerged

Shutting down the surrounding noise.

Everything sounds muffled, like a different language.

I can hear the beating of my heart,

The heat causing it to beat faster.

It sounds so loud and alive under here.

Watching the rise and fall of my chest.

Finally, I can hear myself breathe. ♡

7.
Water Love

By your side in my happy place
The frantic river flows
Gushing
Rushing.
You're fierce today after last night's storm,
Uprooting everything that crosses your path,
Growing and gaining in strength,
Making music like a percussion band.
I could listen to you play all day,
Sat here next to you on the cool damp land.

Breathing in your immense changing beauty,
I love being here with you!
Your splashing spray touches my skin –
It feels like a thousand tiny ice shards.
Feeling the earthy connection between us,
Helping to clear the fog in my head.
My arms outstretched,
Cleansing my heart and my soul.
You make me feel so alive,

Bringing me such inner peace and stillness.

The ducks bravely riding your white waters.
I'd love to immerse myself in you
But your depths
Your darkness
Your murky black ripples
Fill me with so much fear.
I'm scared to even dip my toe.
You might uproot me too
Then I'm lost in your flow,
Laid to rest on your watery bed.
I have so much respect for you,
More than you have for me,
Yet I love you. ♡

8.
Goodbye Mum

Taken from us at such short notice

Without any warning!

It was too soon.

We had plans.

I'd been talking to you earlier, you were fine.

You were getting ready to go dancing –

You loved to dance!

Only hours later the phone call arrived.

You'd been rushed into hospital.

The doctor said you wouldn't see the night out.

I felt sick!

Every bit of me ached for your touch.

Was it all just a really bad dream?

My worst nightmare.

How could this be happening to you?

You were far too young.

You can't leave me, leave us, your family.

I had to give you one last hug,

To tell you I loved you one last time.

I needed to tell you what a wonderful mum you had

been.

How I appreciated everything you'd ever done for me.

How proud I was to call you my mum.

And how I was truly going to miss my best friend.

I breathed in your essence for the very last time –

I would hold that smell in my heart forever.

Never would I forget what you smelt like.

Never would I forget what you looked like.

I see you every time I look in the mirror.

It was time to say goodbye, I wasn't ready.

But you were.

You had to leave,

Ready to begin your next chapter.

I place one last kiss on your beautiful soft skin. ♡

9.
You Made My Day

You smiled at me across a crowded room.
Our eyes lit up as they met
And later we fell in love.
It was a beautiful moment,
One that I will never forget.
You made my day.

You smiled at me as we walked by the lake.
We were strangers.
We said hello to each other,
We talked about the weather,
And walked a while together.
You made my day

You smiled at me as you sat on the cold floor asking for money
I smiled back and sat with you.
We chatted for a while.
People walked past us
Not even casting a glance

Like we didn't even exist.
You are the same as the other strangers I met.
You are one I will never forget.
And you made my day. ♡

10.
Nothing Has Changed

The world is still revolving, time hasn't yet stood still,
It's just some of the memories that are starting to dilute.
The season's they have been and gone
Yet things remain the same.

In a sky of black and orange the moon appears again,
Still there in all its glory, a mesmerising sight,
Wearing a scarf of swirling wispy clouds
And a scattering of twinkling lights.

The sun still rises high each day in the morning sky
Hiding behind a thick haze of many shades of grey,
Waiting shyly to show its bright glowing face
To warm us with a gentle heat.

The lake still holds such mystery of what lies beneath,
Covered in delicate pink blossom stolen by the breeze.
The Willow trees are taller now, bending over gently,
Tips dipping the water as they weep.

In the deep depths of the forests under a canopy of leaves
Amongst the undergrowth, young deer frolic for all of us to see.
The foot paths barely visible, hidden under moss
The smell of vegetation never to be lost.

In my thoughts you are always there, never too far from reach
My mind and heart letting go, swaying, ebb and flow.
A stroll in nature's garden, the birds and the bees
Yet things remain the same.

There was you.
And now there is just me. ♡

Start each day with
a grateful heart

11.
Romantic Day For One

The ocean waves lap gently at my feet
As I paddle in ankle deep
With love by my side
The feel of the soft wet sand between my toes,
The reflection of the sun mirrored on the sea
Makes me close my eyes to see the beauty that lies ahead.
My hair is blowing wild, thick with salty sea air.
Taking a deep breath in, it helps to clear my head.

Gazing at the fluffy light cotton wool clouds,
The shapes they form horizon bound,
The shiny orange jelly fish washed upon the shore
Make me dance on feet of air.
Seagulls screeching loudly
Riding the bumpy thermals,
Poised, ready to swoop on unsuspecting diners –
They're about to steal their food

Dogs bark with excitement, tentatively waiting to play,
Ready to chase their ball the length of the beach.

Kids running wild and free
Burning off boundless amounts of energy,
Parents watching guardedly
Whilst taking time out to recharge.
Couples walking hand in hand carrying their shoes,
The romance of the beach as they gently steal a kiss.

Then there's me.
Alone.
With my thoughts, a note book and a pen.
A gentle breeze to turn my page
Whilst I sit on my crumpled towel amongst the dunes
Looking out towards the sea,
Toes buried in the cool damp sand.
No one else to consider,
Just me and my flask of homemade celery soup. ♡

12.
The Scary Path

I love to immerse myself in nature.
I especially love to be amongst the trees,
I love their energy,
I love how they have the strength to weather any storm.
There's a path in the woods,
It's a lonely route, where not many venture,
A dense wooded darker path that fills me with fear.
Whenever I walk past it, there's a pull to go down it.
I've wanted to walk it so many times to see what the attraction is
But fear always gets the better of me
And I choose the safe path, the one I've always chosen.
Well, yesterday I stared in the face of fear
And I took the scary path.
I could hear my heart pounding in my chest
But there was nothing to fear.
Love had been trying to guide me here for so long,
She wanted me to witness the awesomeness
Of being alone in my favourites space –
The beautiful carpet of golden leaves,

The setting sun casting shadows of the trees,
Their mossy trunks soft on my face as we shared many an embrace.
The thick mud squelched beneath my feet.
It was slippery and ankle deep in places
But I got through it and I loved it.
I continued walking on this new found path,
Absorbing all the life that surrounded me,
Breathing in the fragrant fresh air.
When I reached the end I turned round and walked back
And then I did it again.
And again.
There was no fear anymore,
Just pure love for what I love.
This time, love had conquered fear. ♡

13.
The Raven

What brings you here again, raven?
This isn't your territory.
You've been visiting me every day for a while now,
Looking through the window, rasping and cawing.
You seem so strong and fearless,
Chasing off any daring intruder,
Perching yourself on the spindly branches of the young willow tree,
Becoming unbalanced by the slightest of breeze,
Flapping your purply black wings to steady yourself.
You remind me of Count Dracula,
Wearing an eccentric velvety feathery cape.
You're not like the other birds,
You are magical and mysterious.
Some say you are a bad omen,
A sign of witchcraft and death,
Not of my death
But the death of something that surrounds me,
Something that is coming to an end.
Maybe you're my animal spirit guide

And you're here to keep me on the right path,
Guiding me through these imminent changes.
Through my ripening manifestations
The clues and connections are there,
I just need to recognise and action them.
One day, I will be strong and fearless like you.
One day, I too will fly. ♡

14.
No Fear

Standing on the edge

Ready to unmask fear yet again,

The last street light disappearing behind me.

Guided by the light of the moon

The eerie dark path opened up in front of me.

Fear led the way, whilst love held my hand.

All l could see was the warped silhouettes of the trees

And the glare from my head torch.

It was so quiet,

Not even the bird's muttered.

I headed up the darkened path.

It was a beautiful clear evening,

The night sky was as black as coal

And peppered with a thousand glittering stars.

I continued on the muddy path

Constantly looking behind me

For the monster's hiding in the bushes,

Allowing fear to jump out at me, testing my strength.

Onwards I trudged up the hill,

Finally reaching the crest,

Stopping to take in the view and catch my breath.
The view was absolutely spectacular –
A carpet of multi-coloured flickering lights lay ahead
As far as my eyes could see.
Admiring now the beauty of the dark, as I do the light.
With every breath I took came peace,
My soul coming home,
Resting in this dark fearful place where fear no longer resides.
Fear and Love held hands on the way back down,
Proud of their achievement. ♡

15.
Oh, to Be a Woman

Oh, to be a woman

When you get to a certain age –

When the menopause starts to hit you

And the sweat runs down your face,

Time of the month is upside down

Not arriving when it should

Those persistent hot sweats

Come in a torrent of rage,

Waking you up in the early hours

Feeling like you've stepped out of a shower,

The constant need to blot your face

Just when you've finished you're makeup

And you're ready to head out.

A stream of sweat trickling down your back,

The ever expanding waistline

That exercise and diet just won't shift,

A wardrobe full of clothes but none of them will fit.

Hot flushes like an internal furnace –

You feel you're about to combust.

Maybe they start at your tummy

Or maybe begin at your feet,
Rising up through your body
With an unexplainable heat
Heading straight for your face.
Mood swings like a roller coaster rush,
Emotional highs and lows,
Crying and not knowing why,
Feelings of frustration and anger,
Your libido a thing of the past.
Oh ,and don't forget forgetfulness,
Another of the signs.
You'll need to keep a diary for events dates and times.
Next time you're in a crowd of people,
Just take a look around.
The poor woman sat there fanning her face
And beads of sweat running down her brow
With a fresh rosy glow on her cheeks.
Please don't be shy, come and say, "Hi."
That person is probably me! ♡

16.
My Girl

A wonderful mummy you have become
Single-handedly running your home
Doing things your way
How you think is best
Working hard to feather your nest
Giving your daughter the very best you can
Proving in life you don't need a man
Teaching your little girl right from wrong
Showing her how to play
Baking together
And teaching her songs
Opening her eyes to the beautiful world
To nature, the sunset, the magnificent moon
Walking for miles in the great outdoors
Things that cost nothing, what's not to love?
Her life she'll look back on as she grows up
Her knowledge
Her empathy
Her self-belief
Self-trust

Self-worth

Self-love

She'll know that it came from her mummy's true love. ♡

17.
Willow

Watching my little granddaughter

Sat playing on the floor

Toys all around her

No room for anymore

Still wearing her pyjamas

Dried breakfast on her chin

Long brown curly hair

Piled high upon her head

I love how she calls me Nannie

Her little voice so sweet

She's beautiful

Has sparkly blue eyes

And soft pure olive skin

She loves to sing and dance around

Wearing a frilly princess dress

And a pink diamante crown

Her connection with love

Already strong

The empathy she shows at such a tender age

I love you, little one, I hope you never change. ♡

18.
Just a Little Walk

It's only a mile and a half you said

Rucksack packed should be back for tea

Climbing up rocks

Looking out to the sea

Opening gates

Striding the styles

Stopping to take selfies

Working that smile

Admiring the goats

With their big curly horns

Oh, these boots are rubbing my corns!

Not far now

Trudging through puddles thick with mud

Overgrown footpaths

Watch out for the slugs

Butterflies and bees

Settling on flowers

Stopping to eat blackberries every few seconds

Crossing the water

On slippery rocks

I think I've developed a hole in my sock.

Almost there now

Dark clouds are gathering, it's started to rain

I forgot my coat

I'm getting soaked

Stinging nettles

Hawthorn hedges

My aching legs are now covered in scratches

There's a stone in my shoe

I'm in need of the lco

There's only another mile and a half to go.

19.
The Visitor

Something woke me in the early hours,
The darkness of the room blending
With the dark moonless night.
There's a presence here,
A presence that I've felt before,
Sharing with me this still dark night.
I have nothing to fear,
Love is here with me.
Rubbing my eyes to focus
I'm struggling to see anything.
There's a smell,
It's familiar, I've smelt it before.
I recognise it but can't yet place it.
I feel your presence coming nearer.
It feels like you're sitting on my bed,
I feel there's a dip at my feet.
I wish you were near the window,
There's a tiny chink of light –
Maybe I could see you there.
I feel you're by my face now

But I can't feel you breathe,
I can't hear your heart.
I know you're there
Gently stroking my hair,
Touching my face.
I know that it's you, Mum,
An angel for far too many years,
Never too far away,
Always by my side
When I have a troubled mind.
I wake in the morning only to find
One single white feather that you've left behind! ♡

20.
My Boy

I watch you with your baby girl

So tender

So gentle

And loving

Showering her with kisses

Enveloping her with love

Already the perfect daddy

You've changed so much these last few years

You've always been my little boy

Now you've become a lovely man

One that I respect so much

For not sticking to the plan

Listening to your heart

You knew things would be tough

Look at you now

How life has changed

With a baby of your own

A proper family man

I'm proud to say you're my son. ♡

"One of the ego's favourite paths of resistance is to fill you with doubt."

~ Ram Dass

21.
A Stolen Moment

Watching a loving couple

As I sit here on the beach

I feel like I'm intruding but they're there for all to see

Just a stolen moment

Snuggled up close on a little towel

She leans into him

Her head resting on his arm

He kisses her gently on her head

Then slips his arm around her waist

Pulling her in closer

He's whispering something in her ear

Giggling like children

His hand gently stroking her back

Gently touching her sunburnt skin

She reacts with a shudder of pleasure

And she turns to look at him

Their eyes lock

Solitude

Like there's no one here but them

He licks his lips and goes in for a kiss

His fingers running through her hair
She's holding his face in her hands
Suddenly she pulls away
As a voice shouts out loud
Eeewww stop that it's disgusting
Their kids are back with an ice cream.

22.
All Hallows Eve

A full moon is set to rise

On this Hallows Eve

The most magical night of the year

When the veil is thin

Between the two worlds

Of the living and the dead

Candles burning flickering bright

In pumpkin faces they light up the night

Guiding lost souls back to their home

When you're walking the streets you won't be alone

Dressed up in your costumes

With fake blood and fangs

That zombie you passed, he's there right behind you

Watch out for the bats circling above

It might just be vampire thirsty for blood

While covens of witches sit huggled around

Stirring their cauldrons with

Recipes of old

Calling out to all the lost souls

Tonight's the night you better beware

When you hear a noise that's under the stairs

That creaking floor board

The slamming of a door

That strange little noise you haven't heard before

So when you go to bed tonight

Get under the covers

Keep your feet tucked in tight

You never know who's watching

Waiting

In the still of the night

Patiently waiting

Until you to turn out the light. ♡

23.
The Dream

I dreamt about world peace
No more bombs
Or bloodshed
No more shattered lives
No more guns or knife crime
Men and women coming together
Hugging, kissing, shaking hands
Sharing a beer, a laugh and a joke
Reassuring each other of our darkest fears
Talks of peace and rebuilding our lives
Sat together side by side
Blood stained hand in hand.

I dreamt about world hunger
No more starving people
All sitting down to eat dinner
Around a great big wooden table
More food than we can dream of
No more rumbling tummies
A clean clear glass of water

Clothes on our backs
And shoes on our feet
A steady flow of rain
To help us all to grow crops
Enjoying being self-sufficient.

I dreamt about homelessness
An end to sleeping rough
No more begging on the streets
A place we can all call our home
A nice safe place to sleep
A bed and a pillow to rest our head
A job to go to every day
Giving us a purpose
With food in our cupboards
Money in our pockets
Enjoying the sound of it jingle.

I dreamt about child abuse
No more children living in fear
Hiding under the bed
Or in the cupboard under the stairs.
Being innocent like a child should
Never afraid to speak our truth
Freedom to run and play

Laughing having fun
Riding our bike with the wind in our hair
Not a care in the world
And never afraid of going home.

I dreamt about animal cruelty
Finally an end to their suffering
Making a stand fighting for their rights
We had to be their voice
It worked, it stopped
No more baiting of cats and dogs
Exploiting unusual breeds
Foxes no longer chased through fields
By crazed humans in red jackets on horse back
An end to poaching of wildlife
No more trophy killing
Extinction no longer a threat

If only my dreams would come true
To live in peace and harmony
All people and creatures great and small. ♡

24.
Florence

Welcome to our world little one

Thank you for choosing us

A special gift she's sent with love

She's perfect

A precious girl with diamond eyes

Ten tiny fingers

Ten tiny toes

A beautiful little button nose

A full head of hair

Her face so full of grace

Her soft peachy skin

With little milky spots

Lying there in her tiny cot

Wrapped up in her blankets

Her hat a little big

Adapting to life already

She's taking everything in

Bonding with her parents

The aroma of her their skin

Getting to know their voices

Their reassuring words
Their delicate touch
A lifetime of lessons
An eternity of blessings
Our little girl will always be cherished
And swaddled in arms of love. ♡

25.
The Storm

A wild storm is brewing
They warned us that it would
It's needed to cool the earth's crust

I can hear it rumbling in the distance
Letting out an enormous roar
Like a thousand wild horses, galloping over the moors
Like tumbling waves crashing
Splitting the ocean floor
The tidal swell of a stormy sea
The rising ebb and flow

I can see it now in all its glory
Illuminating the sky
Like a bright summer's day at night
Flashing and flickering like a ball of disco lights
Dancing amongst the clouds
An iridescent blue haze
Sending flashes across the sky,
A dazzling blinding white light

I can feel it now coming closer

The intense heat of the day

Gradually starting to fade

The rustling of the leaves as the breeze comes out to play

Rain becoming heavier dampening the day

Flowing like a rapid stream falling over rocks

The smell, oh the smell, nature's earthy delight. ♡

26.
Perfect Timing

The rain woke me up in the early hours
I lay and listened to it falling on the roof
And trickling down the tiles
Sweet music to my ears
It was so peaceful
Just me and the rain
No other distractions
No outside noise
No nagging voices in my head
Telling me to get up out of bed
They were still asleep
Perfect time to meditate
Perfect me time
Just me, love and the rain. ♡

27.
Messages From Love

Sat here in the garden

On the rickety old wooden bench

It's creaking, groaning and protesting

Under the weight of me

Kicking off my shoes I plant my feet on the grass

Taking in a few deep breaths to smell the summery air

The sweet scent of flowers

My washing blowing on the line

And meaty barbecues

I close my eyes to rest a while

Ahh this is the life

The chorus of the birds becoming distant

The laughter of the kids becoming faint

The rustle of trees restrained

Drifting in and out of sleep

The dream begins again

Standing in front of a great huge wall

Covered in letters and notes

I don't recognise the writing, I haven't seen it before

Don't be afraid to ask for more

You are now visible for all to see
Embrace not define
Trust your higher self
There's freedom on the other side
Feel the abundance of love
Gratitude, always gratitude
Gently, there comes a soft warm breeze
My nose starts to tingle with the smells
Slowly the wall starts to fade
No, not yet, I haven't finished reading
I wake from my nap sat here in the garden
On the rickety old wooden bench. ♡

28.
Spring Equinox

The Spring Equinox has arrived,
Light and dark in equal parts.
I love this time of year.
It's time to wake those creaking bones,
They've been stuck under wraps for months,
Wrapped up in great big jumpers.
Feet stuck in thick woolly sock and boot
In central heated houses
With artificial light.
As the days begin to get longer
Our Mother Earth will wake from her sleep,
Stretching her roots, turning the soil.
Nature will come back to life –
The bright yellow daffodils will spring into bloom,
Buds and leaves on spindly tree branches providing shelter for many,
Dandelions standing tall and proud,
Daisies and buttercups forming a carpet lawn,
Spring lambs frolicking in the fields.

A strong promise of sunshine awaits
Along with the rain,
Life's drink of life for all. ♡

29.
To-Do List

Breathe,

Stay positive

Avoid the news

Eat well

Look after yourself

Read that old book catching dust on the shelf

Paint a picture

Spend time in nature

Study the crossword in yesterday's paper

Call a friend

Send a text

A well-earned nap with the cat on my lap

Tend to the borders

Mow the lawn

Chat with the neighbours over the wall

Sit in the garden

The dark night sky

Gazing at the moon, a shooting star flying by

A little drop of brandy

Medicinal of course

Helps with lubrication when you feel a little hoarse

Time for bed

Sweet dreams and sleep tight

May your tomorrow be filled with love. ♡

30.
Beautiful Women

Love your beautiful body be it curvy or slim.
Love your wobbly belly,
Your stretch marks and varicose veins.
So what if you've got cellulite,
Saggy boobs or a big bum?
Don't spend your life worrying,
It will only make you glum.
Love your dark circles
And crow's feet around your eyes.
Love the creases round your lips,
And disappearing lip line.
So what if you've got wrinkles,
A double chin or two?
Don't spend your life worrying,
It will only make you blue.
Beautiful women we are, through and through
Those perfect imperfections are just what makes you,
You. ♥

"The heart surrenders everything to the moment. The mind judges and holds back."

~ Ram Dass

31.
So Ill

I just want to sleep.
I feel so deprived of it
Yet I've done nothing but sleep
For hours,
For days even.
Just stuck to my bed,
Woven into its springs.
I can't move.
I don't want to move –
It hurts too much.
Feeling like I've been hit by a truck,
Woken occasionally by my cat
With a gentle paw then a head butt,
Wanting me to play or feed him,
Wondering why I've slept more than he does.
it's like he understands
As he settles and snuggles in,
Cramping banging echoes from my tummy
Like an over stretched goat skin drum.
I don't have the energy to eat.

I need to hydrate, but I can barely drink.
Everything takes so much effort.
Sweat pouring out of me like holes in a sieve,
Cradling my clammy aching head in my hands,
Willing the pain to go away,
Leave me alone.
I woke this morning –
It felt like pain has started to listen.

32.
Lucky to Be Here

I've never felt so poorly yet I still didn't listen.
For weeks I was ill before I took notice,
My body screaming at me that it needed help,
Feeding it with over the counter drugs.
It was going into shock,
Shivering like I was naked out in the snow,
Yet a furnace burning in my tummy forcing sweat out of every pore,
My body in unexplainable pain.
I was in Cyprus, I had to get home.

I slept most of the flight, my body taking on the rest,
Preparing for the fight ahead.
The plane landed –
I'd made it!
I took myself to hospital
Yet more rules of controlling the covid virus –
I had to go alone.
I needed emergency surgery –
A ruptured appendix.

It was gangrene,
The contents of which stuck to my colon and bowel,
The toxins seeping into my blood
And the cherry on top an abscess to add to the mess,

The anxiety was overwhelming,
No one here to reassure me,
To tell me I was going to be alright.
I could feel the blood rushing through my veins,
My heart pounding for all to hear.
Was this the end of the road for me?
What if I died during surgery?
I hadn't said my goodbyes to my loved ones,
Never to give them hug or a kiss,
Never to tell them how much I loved them
and how proud they made me feel.
I can't leave, not yet, I'm not ready!

I prayed, *please don't take me*,
I wasn't sure who I was asking,
Just anyone who was listening.
Was this going to be the very last day that I drew breath?
Was this going to be the last journey
On this cold metal bed into theatre?
Into a brightly lit sterile room

Full of people in scrubs,
I can only see their eyes.
The last words I hear –
Count to five
One
Two…

Groggy, I can hear voices.
Are they voices of angels?
I was still in pain but a different pain.
Yes, I had made it!
The surgeon resting his hand on my shoulder
Softly said I was a very lucky lady, lucky to be alive.
I don't know who was listening to my prayers that day
But whoever it was,
To you I am eternally grateful. ♡

33.
Morning Gratitude

Opening my eyes this morning after a lovely restful sleep
On my nice comfortable bed and my lovely soft pillow
The sleep it helped clear my head
My body now feels rested, no aches, pains, or creaking bones
Ready to face the new day and whatever it may hold
The soft gentle breeze coming through the open window
Caressing, cool to the touch on my skin
The bird song, how beautiful they sing at such an early hour
The view I have of the willow tree, it's dancing all around
My cat is purring, after a cuddle, I love to hear that sound
My health, wealth and happiness
My family and my friends
The abundant love we share
The confidence to be vulnerable, writing, speaking my truth
Last but not least, my beating heart giving me new life each day
So full of love, so much love to share

For all of this I give gratitude. ♡

34.
We Are One

Lying here in your arms
Is the best place in the world
Your gentle touch
Your lovely lips
The way they press on mine
Your soft voice saying *I love you*
Sends tingles down my spine
Your whirlpool eyes
Your loving gaze
Burns deep into my soul
Your beautiful naked body
Soft skin on skin
Your heart in sync with mine
Wrapped up in each other's arms
Our bodies completely entwined
This feeling is so sublime. ♡

35.
Message From a Friend

I hear you're moving on

She knew he would eventually

She said it hurts so much

It stings

Like salt in an open wound

A massive void in her chest

That would take some time to heal

She knew that you were hurting too

She knew how much you loved her

She just didn't have the courage to move on herself

The courage to move forward

Take that leap of faith

It doesn't mean she's a coward

Fear held her back

Fear of the unknown

Fear of the future

So you ended it

And she let you go

She wonders if she'll live her life with regret

She tells me you've stayed friends

Since you broke up
She said there hasn't been a single day
That you haven't been in her thoughts
Now she thinks about you even more
She said it's hard
Knowing that you're in someone else's arms
There's someone else on her side of your bed
There's someone else sitting in her place on your sofa
Snuggling up with you
That you're holding someone else's hand
Making plans
Taking your new love to places where you took her
She knows eventually you'll be saying
Those three little words
She said you said it so often to her
Anyway, she knows you're not hers to love anymore
She has to move on, too
She said she'll always hold you in her heart
And that you shared something very special
She said to say she will always love you
And she'll think about you every day. 🖤

36.
Not Today

I was struggling to get out of bed this morning

I could have stayed there all day

Cocooned in the safety of my duvet

Ignorance is bliss

Love has arrived

Don't make me get up and face the world

Not today

Come on, love says

Get in the shower, wash the feelings away

Standing in the solitude of the tiny steamy space

Feeling the warmth of the lovely soft water

Washing over my bruised naked body

I stand for what feels like hours

Cleansing my mind

Drowning my thoughts

Allowing my heart to open

I can cry in the shower

Cry unseen

Unheard

My tears mixing with the flowing water

Love says, *let them flow girl*

Set them free

Standing

Watching

The water and my tears

Together swirling round the drain

Thank you, love, for showing up again. ♡

37.
The Break Up

Why is life so hard sometimes?

Why can't I just cut off from it all?

I want to detach myself

But I can't,

I won't.

What sort of person would that make me?

I'm piggy in the middle

Bouncing back and forth.

Trying to be the glue

That is no longer sticky.

My fibres are stretched to breaking point.

It's taking up valuable headspace

Where there just isn't room.

I need to clear some space.

Trying not to give advice,

Just to be there for them both.

Such a beautiful couple.

I thought they had it all,

The world at their feet.

All this hurt,

Sadness and tears,

Like a bereavement in the family.

Picking up the pieces,

So many pieces missing

Of such young broken love.

38.
I'm Just Tired

Not enough hours in a day

Suppression

Compression

Depression

Weekend came and went

I missed it

Trying to please everyone

Except myself

Guilt

Doubt

Defence

I'm tired of it all

I can't breathe

I can't think

Is it just a phase?

Or a phase of the moon? ♡

39.
A Mother's Love

I dreamt about my mum last night

It all seemed very real

I wasn't the age that I am now

Merely just a child

The feel of her soft warm skin

The smell of her perfume

Her gentle voice reassuring

Whenever I was upset

Tucking my stray wavy hair behind my ears

She would wipe away my tears

With a floral cotton handkerchief

Removed from up her sleeve

A bit of spit to wipe my bloody knee

A kiss on each cheek

A pat on my head

One of those lovely mummy hugs

Sending me back off out to play

All fixed and repaired

Ready to face the world. ♡

40.
The Funeral

Sat amongst the mourners

Mourning their deceased

The end of a life journey

That seems hard to believe

Humanist celebrant reading aloud

Red-eyed faces looking back in the crowd

Sad words said

Causing more tears

Talk of the happy times over the years

A celebration of their life

Someone's husband

Someone's wife

Someone's son

Someone's daughter

Sister, brother

Father, Mother

Being strong, trying not to cry

Coming together to say our goodbye

A picture of them on the coffin it stands

In their best clothes

Looking happy and grand
A lasting memory we now have of you
As we all walk outside to your favourite tune
Standing around in the cold and rain
Shaking hands
Hugging
Revealing our pain
Family and friends we've not seen for years
All stood together drying our tears
Off to the wake to celebrate the life lost
Raising our glasses
Sharing a toast. ♡

If you want the moon…
do not hide at night.
If you want a rose…
do not run from the thorns.
If you want love…
do not hide from yourself.

~ Rumi

41.
The Little Things

Today I finally broke free from the confines of the house.

Off into the big wide world again.

For a walk along the canal,

All on my own.

Well, love came too.

My first taste of freedom for weeks,

At a much slower pace than normal

But I was out, and it felt brilliant.

Everything looked so much brighter,

Crisper and sharper somehow,

Like the lenses of my eyes had been cleaned.

It was like I could see every single blade of grass,

Every vein on every leaf,

And every feather on the swans.

The smell of the ferns,

The trees,

And the sun baked earth.

The smell of the water in the warm sun.

Everything smells so different,

Much more pungent and fragrant.

The canal looked so inviting

I wanted to jump in,

swim over to the heron

And bid him good morning.

The sensation and the sound of the gravel path

Crunching under my feet,

I could feel every tiny stone.

Some hurt,

But in a good way.

It felt fantastic!

I felt so alive!

All that love talked about was

The little things in life. ♡

42.
Unconditional Love

Emptiness.

I feel nothing.

Just devoid.

Of love.

Of hate.

For me that is.

Where are you, love?

I can't feel you?

Who am I?

Why me?

On this journey

This path

I have no passion.

No purpose.

The fire in my belly.

Merely charred smouldering ash.

Just existing.

Not living.

I want to feel

Abundant.
Brimming.
Of life.
Of love.
For me, that is.
Love is calling,
I'm here, I didn't leave.
Come, sit in my silence and listen.
You know who you are,
This is the life you chose.
You chose to embrace this journey
Before you were born.
You are strong enough to follow this path.
I feel that passion returning.
I'm learning to understand my purpose.
The fire in my belly starting to reignite,
Those embers that remained becoming an inferno.
Loving living my existence in this human body
And my lust for life rekindled.
Feeling love's presence every second of every day,
That beautiful inner love,
The one that's unconditional. ♡

43.
Mixed Bag

It's okay to feel flat sometimes,

To be ok, but not to be ok.

I'm not sure how I feel today,

Just a real mixed bag.

Emotions are high,

Tears are sat pending –

If I let them go I will need a boat.

Sadness and excitement at the same time.

Also guilt.

Guilt for feeling happy,

For wanting to be happy.

Love is sat with me

Keeping me company.

Not pushy,

Never pushy.

Just patiently waiting,

Ready to be my cheerleader

With her pompoms,

Or ready to pass me the tissues

And paddle the boat. ♡

44.
Free Spirit

I wanted to escape

To feel freedom

To feel exhilarated

And see beauty

Love took me on a journey

Close your eyes and breathe, she said

Galloping across the acres of moors

On a beautiful dapple grey horse

With eyes of gold

His mane and tail as black as coal

Feeling his racing heart as I held onto him

He carried my weight with ease

His thunderous heavy hooves

As they pound the damp earth

His pace quickening with every stride

Fills me with exhilaration

The long dewy grass whips at my feet

The wind in my face, it catches my breath

Seeing the world through different eyes

No saddle or reins to burden your load

Untamed and free to run and roam

I feel your spirit

Your spirit is me

Running our race against the dark clouds

Heading towards a new day rising sun. ♡

45.
November

Welcome back, November

It's been a while

You make your return in a windy style

Whistling a blustery wintery tune

Than that of the summery month of June

Near naked trees dance on your breeze

Kaleidoscopic colours of falling leaves

Giving shelter to God's tiny creatures

As they forage turning the soil

The river's they run fast and deep

And willow trees stand tall and weep

Before the imminent December freeze

Whilst me and love

Will walk and reap

The beauty of the earth's restful sleep

The magical time of death and rebirth. ♡

46.
Our Jinx

When I was a child we had a cat named Jinx

He was a beautiful big ginger Tom

He wasn't like a normal cat

Roaming the streets and not coming home

He was more like a baby brother

We dressed him up in our dolls' clothes

A cardigan, some mittens and a nice frilly hat

Tied up with a pretty little bow

We'd take him out for a ride in our Silvercross pram

With the hood pulled up to keep off the wind

Me and my sister, quite proud of ourselves

Would take turns in pushing him round

People would stop us to take a look

Expecting to see a baby

Oh, what a shock

When they saw it was not

It was our Jinx

The big ginger cat looking right back

Wearing a cardigan, some mittens and a nice frilly hat

Tied up in a pretty little bow. ♡

47.
Full Moon

The full moon is here again
Making me feel our of sorts.
It's so beautiful, powerful and mysterious,
Reaping such havoc on me,
Feeding the seed in my head and
Causing so much turmoil.
Forcing my hand to make life changes
I've been procrastinating about for years.
Causing me such self-doubt
And self-loathing.
Expanding my problems to breaking point.
I'm not strong enough to fight.
My head is banging to the beat of your drum.
I'm tired yet I can't sleep, you won't let me.
You have so much energy around you.
You drain me completely of mine.
Leaving me lifeless and confused. ♡

48.
The Great Oak Tree

How long have you been standing there?
You must have been there for years.
Every chance I get, I admire you.
We've shared so many hugs.
Your majestic beauty.
Your energy is so empowering,
You share it in abundance.
The elements don't bother you –
You dance in the storm like a free spirit
And you bask in the sunshine.
So many beautiful faces hidden in your trunk.
Your branches span a huge canopy
Offering protection for any passers-by be it man or beast.
I wonder how many people have sat at your roots
Seeking your shade, a place to rest,
To sit with their thoughts
And share a kiss.
Messages of love carved in your flesh –
I hate how that's been done to you.
There forever like a tattoo you didn't want. ♡

49.
An Ode to Mr Fly

I opened the door but you wouldn't leave

I warned you that you were in danger

But you took no notice

Didn't you want your freedom?

Why don't you just go?

You think that I can't see you

Hiding behind the door

You think that I can't hear you

But I've heard that noise before

Don't touch my skin

You're making me feel sick

Don't you touch my food

Stop spreading your germs

Stop teasing the cat, you're being mean

And now you come into my bedroom

Whilst I'm trying to sleep

Rummaging around on my bedside table

There's nothing on there for you

I tried to save you from your fate

I realise now it's far too late

You're there

On your back

Floating In my glass of water

Little stiff legs pointing up to the sky

Your body a beautiful shimmering blue

Your wings of lace, they buzz no more

Your tiny eyes so huge

I tried to warn you, Mr Fly

I opened the door but you wouldn't leave! ♡

50.
Listen to Love

I was awake before the birds today

Everything was still

Nothing stirring apart from me

And my head chatter

Listening to love

Love said *it's time*

Time to love me

Time to set myself free

Break free from the things that hold me back

Keeping me stagnant

All the sadness

Anger

Shame

And stress

That I've let build up

Storing it in my body for so long

Allowing it to fester

There's no room

Carrying these heavy feelings around with me

Hanging onto them for years

Like old clothes that don't fit any more
But you keep just in case
Not knowing where to start
I'm sure love will guide me
Let the internal work commence. ♡

Each night,
the moon kisses secretly
the lover who counts the stars.

~ Rumi

51.
My Birthday

And so my journey began

On this very day

Wednesday September 30th, 1964

The day I was born into this world

Born to the parents that I'd so carefully chosen

To learn my life lessons

Of patience, compassion and love

I knew it was going to be tough

but I knew they already loved me more than life itself

And I too loved them

Unconditionally

My decision was made

The veil was drawn

And I began my new adventure

Birthed kicking and screaming into this life

Closing my eyes today

I have a strong feeling that I've never noticed before

A strong strange feeling of being reborn

A pressure around my head

Like a heady hangover

A feeling of stillness

Of peace and calm

Yet eagerness and excitement

Of new beginnings

And what lies ahead

Feeling that strong connection to my mum

Even in her passing

The bond that never broke

The bond that never will break until I pass

I feel her presence today stronger than ever

Still teaching me my life lessons

Patience, compassion and love. ♡

52.
My Beautiful Love and Me

My beautiful love and me
Ventured out on a dreamy journey
Floating high in the velvet night sky
Tiptoeing through the stars
Soaring over the snow-capped mountains
Gliding through the deep silent valleys
Riding high on the crest of a wave
Skimming the tranquil moon drenched sea
By the light of the mystical magical moon
We danced on the glittering shimmery sands
Hand in hand
My beautiful love and me. ♡

53.
Time to Go

I've never been good at goodbyes

But it was time to go

To leave my son and his little family behind in Cyprus

I gave my son a last loving breath stopping hug

I didn't want to let him go

I could feel his soft beard on my face

Reminding me my little boy now a grown man

With a beautiful little baby girl

And a family of his own

I miss him so much

I told him I loved him

And he returned the love

And my heart absorbed it with tears

And off he went to work

I held my beautiful precious granddaughter

And fed her one last time

Our love already an immensely strong bond

I placed a gentle kiss on her soft peachy face

And tightly held her in my arms

Looking at her so tiny and so perfect

I thanked her for choosing us

And asked love to keep her safe

We drove to the airport

The three girls

Full of chat love and laughter

The journey went so quickly

Yet another goodbye

We held each other tightly

No need for any words

We felt the exchange of love between us

The beautiful young woman who loves my son

Almost as much as I did

The wonderful mum to my granddaughter

I know she is guided by love too

I waved them off

Love sat with me and held my hand all the way home. ♡

54.
I'm Grounded

I'm grounded by the virus
It's like being a child all over again
Banished to the house
No one wants to play with me because I've got the lurgy
Don't go near her you'll catch it.
Watching friends walk past my house
Holding hands and laughing
Riding their bikes, wearing their jazzy helmets
Running as fast as they can in their new funky trainers
Going out for a ride in their nice shiny car
They don't notice me sat by the window
Longingly watching
While they are all out having fun
And I sit here on my own
I'm not allowed to play out

But when I am allowed to play out
I'm going to skip down the street with my head in the clouds
A smile on my face and love by my side

I'll run as fast as I can, wild, barefoot and free
Even the birds won't keep up with me
I'll ride my bike at phenomenal speeds
With the wind in my hair, enjoying the breeze
With my feet off the pedals
Splashing through deep muddy puddles
I'll go out for a ride in my nice shiny car
To the ends of the earth, we'll travel afar
Just me and love
Making a stop on the way home
For red hot chips, with lashings of salt and vinegar
And we'll sit on the grass and eat them
Fresh from the paper. ♡

55.
Dance With Me Love

Dance with me love
And so she did,
Exquisitely.

Yesterday we danced
In the morning, me and love,
Wearing our pyjamas and bare foot,
Strutting our stuff around the kitchen
Waiting for the kettle to boil.
Like the kettle, I too needed to let off steam.

I turned the music up loud
And I danced.
I danced like no one was watching,
Allowing myself to let go
Of everything that held me back,
Keeping me in contraction,
Allowing myself to be a free spirit.
Me being me
If only for these moments.

My movements flawed and out of time,
My arms and legs flailing
Like a ceremonial tribal dance,
I didn't care.
My body becoming the music
Getting lost in the rhythm.
I could no longer hear the words,
I could only feel the beat and the vibration,
And my heart playing the drums.

At last, my heart In synchronicity with love,
Feeling the expansion in my chest,
Throwing my head back
And laughing out loud.
My heart and love
Becoming a beautiful sequence dancing partnership.
Same time tomorrow, we agree. ♡

56.
Dreamy Day in Cyprus

Walking down the cobbled pavement in Cyprus

Pushing my tiny granddaughter in her pram

It will be a long time before she will appreciate

The beauty that surrounds her

It's stunning here

The elegant silhouettes of the Cypress trees

Standing to attention

Like soldier's on parade

The beautiful delicate flowery fir trees

That are alive with bees

The peace and tranquillity

There's hardly a soul around

I walk along the path looking out to the sea

I stop to rest on a bench

While the little one sleeps

Contentedly

Smiling in her sleep

I wonder what she is dreaming about

The sun is just about to set

It's a beautiful shade of tangerine tinged with red

Slowly sinking, sizzling into the sea
So big and bright you could almost touch it
My mind starts to wander
Thoughts of romance
And love
To be here
Sharing this spectacular sight
Feeling the glow of the sun
Feeling my own inner glow
It gives me a warm fuzzy feeling. ♡

57.
My Beating Heart

Be still my beating heart

What do I put you through?

Filling you with such nonsense

Of romance and love

If onlys

And what ifs

Never giving you any clarity

Or stability for you to build on

Never knowing which way to turn

Yet you keep me strong

You keep me alive

I feel your love for me through every beat of you. ♡

58.
Bonfire Night

Excited kids running home from school.

Bonfire night is here!

Red hot bowl of Tattie hash,

Parkin,

Black peas in a cup,

Chewy treacle toffee sticking to your teeth.

Pink and white marshmallows stuck on a stick.

Grown-ups lighting fireworks

Stored safety in a tin.

Stand back,

Take care,

Be sure that they will go with a bang.

Rockets flying way up high,

With a screech they light up the sky.

All the colours of the rainbow

Shining brightly in the night,

Slowly fading out of sight.

Sparklers glowing spitting sparks,

Writing your name against the dark.

Sat around the bonfire,

Warm faces, glowing cheeks.

Stoking the dancing flames,

Embers glowing

The smell of the smoky night air.

59.
Luscious Lips

I watched his lips as he spoke
I longed for him to rest them on mine
His tongue glancing across them
Occasionally
Inviting me in
I didn't hear a word he said
Love was in my ear,
"Do it, do it!"
Sshhhh, I told her, we're talking.
I wondered if his love was nagging him to do the same
My gaze kept drifting from his eyes to his lips.
Love was back again, egging me on.
"Look at those luscious lips, don't you just –"
Sshhhh. I stopped her in her tracks.
They did look lovely though
All pink and soft and kissable.
Then I realised he'd asked me a question.
I couldn't answer.
I hadn't been listening.
I'd been having a battle to silence love.

He asked again,

"Can I kiss you?"

My heart skipped a beat

As my love and his love high-fived each other. ♡

60.
Strange Feelings

There's a force inside that's stronger than I am.

It's giving me a feeling of vibration

Throughout my body

Yet I feel total relaxation.

It's very unsettling.

It's raising anger

Sadness

And love.

Everything I would normally do and enjoy

Makes me feel agitated.

I can't settle to do anything.

The TV programme that I usually enjoy –

I couldn't stand the sound of their voices.

I tried to write about it,

But my pen wouldn't move on the paper.

I tried to read, but kept reading the same line.

It kept me awake,

Constantly prodding me to turn over

And look out of the window.

Every noise in the night was amplified.

It's a feeling of complete disconnection,
Total disillusion with everything.
It's like the constant flipping of a coin –
Whichever side it lands is how I feel.
In all of this weirdness
There's a deep feeling of being wrapped up in love.
A feeling of warmth,
Of comfort and safety. ♡

61.
Go With the Flow

Acceptance, said love,

You're learning,

It's all about acceptance

Not guilt.

Everything that's happening right now

Is meant to be.

Don't fight the process,

Go with the flow

And enjoy

Whatever will be will be.

So with these thoughts

And love's help

We got to work and painted the walls.

Later we sat with a cup of tea and a hot buttered crumpet

Admiring our handy work. ♡

62.
Drifting Off

There's a blanket of fog descending
As I lay in bed trying to sleep.
It must be cold outside –
There's tiny droplets of water vapour
Condensing at the corners of the windows.
Looking beyond the moisture
It looks like a scene from Sherlock Holmes.
I can just see the tree tops,
They're so still.
Not the smallest of branches moves.
The night is so serene and grey
With an empty sky,
No moon,
No stars,
Just a soft golden haze surrounding the street lights.
I can just see the dark silhouette of the rooftops
Of the houses in the next street.
There's a tall chimney billowing out
Fluffy silver clouds of smoke.
I start to dream,

Sat in front of a roaring fire

Wearing winter socks

With my feet far too close to the flames,

Wriggling my toes.

The warmth is delightful.

A nice cup of hot chocolate

Giving me that nice rosy glow,

My eyes getting heavy in all this cosiness.

Suddenly a barking dog brings me back to my pillow. ♡

63.
Fragile

You can love her
But you can't keep her
You can kiss her
But it won't free her
You can hold her
But don't drop her
She is lost
But you won't find her
Be gentle with her
She's fragile. ♡

64.
Anxiety

Anxious feelings

I've never had them before

I can't explain the feeling

Emptiness

Heavy chest

Shallow breath

I can't breathe

Like a pain that isn't painful

Yet it hurts

A burning sensation

I just feel numb

Here in body

But not heart or mind

My heart is lost

My head is whizzing

I can't think straight

Too many thoughts

Running around my head

Disturbing my night

And now my day

Testing my emotional strength

Energy levels at zero

I thought I'd be okay

But I'm not

But life goes on

Best foot forward

Game show face on

Straighten your mask

Behind it the tears flow

No one will notice. ♡

65.
I Shouldn't Be Here

Standing on the edge of the lake
Watching the dark water gently ripple
I know I shouldn't be here
This is your place, not mine
We often walked together here
Your hand holding mine
Talking of times past
The present
And what may lie ahead
What if you're here, maybe I should leave
Our love no longer lingers here
Those times we had are gone
Eventually as distant as the stars
Disappearing into the universe
Maybe in another life
On Jupiter or Mars. ♡

66.
Time

What time is it?

Time is of the essence.

Be on time.

Have you got time?

Can you make time?

No time to stop.

Time to get up.

Breakfast, dinner and tea time.

Bedtime.

I don't have enough time.

Give your time wisely.

Choose who you spend your time with.

Spend time with people you love.

You can't turn back time.

Time is a priceless precious gift.

Make the most of your time.

Time waits for no man or woman.

Don't waste your time. ♡

67.
Sadness

She lost him yesterday.

My friend's son passed away,

The man you all so kindly prayed for.

Completely consumed by the illness,

He couldn't stay any longer,

Leaving behind heartbreak and sorrow.

His future wife and his baby girl,

His mum, dad and sisters,

Facing a life without him.

Their strong family bond made even stronger,

Totally consumed with grief.

My friend, his mum,

beautiful inside and out,

Desperate to change places with her son.

I have so much love for her.

My heart aches for her loss,

Allowing me and love to share in her grief.

I can't even imagine how she must feel.

Her heart bleeding for the loss of love,

Losing belief in her own love.

I'll sit with her,

And me and my love will hold her. ♡

68.
Summer's End

The man next door is mowing his lawn
Probably the last trim of the year
The blades of the mower are struggling
Under the heavy dampened grass
And the sodden fallen leaves
Cutting through the sticks
Detached from the trees
There's more moss than grass now
I miss seeing the little lawn flowers
And their bright flowery faces
Sitting making daisy chains
With my granddaughter on the lawn
Amongst the sun bright buttercups
And the beautiful dandy dandelions
A carpet of delight
The glorious smell of fresh cut grass
Carried on the autumn breeze
Taking in a deep breath
I close my eyes
And absorb the last dreamy smell of summer.

Printed in Great Britain
by Amazon